OET SPEAKING FOR NURSES BOOK 2

By Virginia Allum

© OET Speaking for Nurses Book 2 by Virginia Allum

2017 All rights reserved

Contents

1. Communication Focus: Encouraging the following of treatment

Scenario: Child with Eczema

2. Communication Focus: Persuading

Scenario: Newborn with Jaundice

3. Communication Focus: Gathering Information to assess Pain

Scenario: Admission to A&E with Back Pain

4. Communication Focus: Giving Advice on Lifestyle

Scenario: High Cholesterol

5. Communication Focus: Reassuring

Scenario: diabetic foot injury

A NOTE ABOUT THE UPDATED OET SPEAKING SUB-TEST

After September, 2018, the OET format for the Listening and Reading Sub-tests will change slightly.

THERE WILL BE NO CHANGE TO THE FORMAT OF THE SPEAKING SUB-TEST, that is, two (2) role plays will be performed, each of 5 minutes duration.

There is a minor change to the assessment of the role plays, in that from September, 2018 the updated OET will also assess clinical communication skills. Clinical communication skills are the skills needed to communicate confidently in the workplace.

Examples of these skills include:
- **relationship building** (helping a patient to feel comfortable, when discussing concerns with you, building a feeling of trust between the nurse and the patient)

- **understanding the patient's perspective** (showing empathy and understanding especially in situations where patients are anxious or worried, e.g. because they do not understand their treatment)

- **providing structure to the conversation** (being able to 'signpost' information, so patients are ready to listen to what is said)

- **establishing what a patient already knows** (working out, whether to build on existing knowledge or start from the beginning, when patients do not have any prior knowledge of their condition or its treatment)

- **gathering information from the patient** (showing a range of questioning skills, confirming information which is unclear and summarising)

The general principles of the role plays remain:

- the candidate (playing the role of a nurse) should always initiate and control the role play

- any medical information needed for the role play should be contained in the role play. If candidates are unsure of a medical term, they should make the best guess of what would be appropriate to say in the context of the role play. For example, if the role play is about a respiratory condition, phrases about breathing, tightness in the chest, coughing or sneezing would be appropriate, where phrases about indigestion or bowel movements would not.

Encouraging the following of treatment

Scenario: Flare Up of Eczema in a Child

Vocabulary

cream

to be drying to the skin

to flare up / a flareup

to be itchy /itchiness

to moisturize the skin / a moisturiser

to scratch / scratching

skin condition

steroids / a steroid cream

weeping

Communication Strategies in the Role Play
- giving advice in a sensitive way
- talking about possible consequences
- encouraging patients to continue treatment
- using patient information leaflets to provide further information

Role Play Themes:
- childhood eczema
- management of the symptoms of skin conditions
- medication used to treat eczema flareups
- patient information leaflets

Talking about Skin Conditions

Think about the terms which might be used in a role play about a skin condition. Some of the skins conditions which might be included in role plays include:

- eczema in a child
- eczema in an adult
- rash of measles or chicken pox
- rash of shingles
- sunburn
- scald (steam burn)
- chemical burn
- petechiae (red spots) of scurvy
- contact dermatitis

Review the terms which might be used:

blister / blistered skin

blotch / blotchy

cracked skin

dry / dryness / dried out

inflammation / inflamed

itchiness / itchy

pimple / pimply

pus / pus-filled

rash / covered in a rash

roughness / rough

a scratch / scratchy

Now, review some treatments you might talk about in the role play:

cream / steroid cream / anti-histamine cream

lotion / dab on lotion

ointment

moisturiser / to moisturise the skin

Setting: Accident and Emergency

Nurse: You are talking to the mother of a child who has had a flareup of her eczema. The child has been scratching her skin, which is now weeping (has a discharge). The mother had refused to use steroid creams, because of concerns about steroids.

Task:
1. Find out about the current skin problem
2. Explain the importance of using moisturising cream
3. Reinforce occasional need for steroid cream
4. Give the mother a leaflet with further information

Communication Strategies used in the Role Play
Giving advice in a sensitive way

During the role play, the nurse often praises the mother for trying to minimise her daughter's symptoms, then offers some advice. For example, the nurse tells the mother that she made the right choice in using unperfumed soap to wash her daughter. Then the nurse suggests that it might be better for the child to have less frequent baths, because hot water can dry the skin.

Nurse: *Yes, it's better to use unperfumed soap, if you have a skin condition like eczema, but it might be better for your daughter not to have a bath every day. Hot water tends to dry out the skin.*

Suggestions, Advice and Strong Advice

The nurse uses a range of suggestions (*It might be a good idea, It would be better to*), advice (*Try to..,* The imperative form, e.g. *Use…)* and strong advice (*It's very important… It's essential that…*)

Watch the video at https://www.youtube.com/watch?v=i3LXUvS1llU

Activity 1: Complete the nurse's sentences:

1. Yes, _____ unperfumed soap, if you have a skin condition like eczema….

2. … but _____ for your daughter not to have a bath every day.

3. Some of these creams can be very good, but _____ remember that they still contain medications.

4. _____ stop severe itching that may lead to the skin bleeding.

5. _____ keep her cool, especially at night. It may make it easier for her to sleep.

6. Also, _____ dress your daughter in clothes made of cotton or natural fibres.

7. _____ cut down on the number of baths your daughter has…

8. _____ put on the moisturising cream several times a day.

9. Finally, _____ the steroid cream for flareups and only as a short-term treatment.

10. _____ it home with you and _____, if you have any further questions.

Talking about possible consequences

During the role play, the nurse explains what might happen, if the mother continues to wash the child every day. He says that washing every day is not a good idea, because, '*Hot water tends to dry out the skin.*'

Using the expression 'tends to' has the effect of softening what the nurse says. He starts by telling the mother she is doing the right thing by using unperfumed soap, then explains that this is not enough to help with the eczema. By being supportive first, the nurse softens the information he gives the mother, as she is concerned that her actions may have worsened her daughter's condition.

Here is the excerpt:

Patient: I give her a bath every morning, so she is clean for the day. I'm always careful to use unperfumed soap. It's supposed to be better for her skin.

Nurse: Yes, it's better to use unperfumed soap, if you have a skin condition like eczema, but it might be better for your daughter not to have a bath every day. Hot water tends to dry out the skin.

The nurse also advises the mother about the consequences of not using the steroid cream prescribed by the GP. He has to be tactful in his explanation, as the mother mentions that she has been doing her own research about the creams on the internet.

The nurse starts by agreeing that some of the creams mentioned on the internet can be helpful, then explains the consequences of not using the cream prescribed by the GP (... it's only to be used now and then, when the condition gets worse. It's important to stop severe itching that may lead to the skin bleeding.)

Here is the excerpt:
Patient: I'm still not happy about it. I was reading about some natural creams on the internet. They're supposed to be very good.
Nurse: Some of these creams can be very good, but it's important to remember that they still contain medications. Your GP has prescribed a cream that she thinks is right for your daughter. And it's only to be used now and then, when the condition gets worse. It's important to stop severe itching that may lead to the skin bleeding.

Using patient information leaflets to provide further information

This role play is an example of where offering to provide a patient education leaflet can be a good way to end the role play.

Patient information leaflets are a good source of information about diseases and conditions. They often give advice on treatment of a condition, as well as simple ways people can manage a condition at home.

Because of this, they provide useful language for giving advice in a role play, as well as offering a way to summarise or 'round off' the role play. When you finish your conversation, offer your patient a leaflet on the topic you have been discussing.

Activity 2: Look at the following example of a Patient Information Leaflet about Eczema.

Managing Eczema: Dos and Don'ts

1. Do keep the bedroom cool
2. Do use cotton or natural fibres (not wool, as it can make itching worse)
3. Don't use perfumed soaps: use special oils or just water
4. Do apply moisturiser frequently during the day and before going to bed
5. Don't wash your skin frequently (it strips your skin of oils)
6. Do wash in tepid rather than hot water (hot water dries skin)
7. Do use small amounts of steroid creams for flareups
8. Don't use steroid creams for long-term use
9. Do keep fingernails short (stops scratching leading to bleeding skin and possible infection)
10. Do be aware of triggers for your eczema, e.g. food (dairy, chocolate and citrus fruit)

Watch the video again and identify the information from the patient information leaflet which was used in the role play by either the nurse or the child's mother.

Write 'Nurse' or 'Mother' next to the example in the role play. The first one is done for you.

1. Nurse
2.
3.
4.
5.
6.
7.
8.
9.
10.

Scenario: Young Mother of a Baby with Jaundice

Vocabulary

bilirubin

jaundice

neonatal

sleepy

tinge

Communication Strategies

- trying to understand the perspective of the patient
- explaining a procedure using everyday language
- reinforcing the importance of treatment
- persuading a patient to remain in hospital

Language Focus

- **diseases and conditions as countable or uncountable nouns**

Look at the nurse's role play card below.

Setting: Maternity Hospital Ward

Nurse: Your patient is an 18-year-old girl who had a baby 3 days ago. The baby is healthy, but has jaundice. The patient would like to be discharged, but needs to stay until the baby's blood test results are known, in case the baby needs treatment for jaundice.

Task:

1. Explain why the patient needs to stay in hospital.

2. Explain jaundice in everyday terms

3. Explain the treatment for jaundice

4. Persuade patient to stay in hospital and reinforce need to stay in hospital

Communication Strategy: Showing that you understand the perspective of the patient

Listen carefully and try to understand what is behind their concerns. Perhaps they are frightened or have been given conflicting information. Respect their right to make decisions about their own healthcare, however much you disagree.

The patient (young mother) starts the role play by saying that she wants to go home. This means that the nurse does not start the role play by finding out more about the problem. Instead, the nurse starts by trying to show that she understands the perspective of the patient, before explaining why the patient needs to stay a bit longer in hospital.

Some of the expressions which can be used to show that you understand are:
I know you don't want to be here, but..
I can see that it's hard for you to have to stay here,
I can appreciate, that you'd rather go home, but...

Explaining a procedure using everyday language

When you are planning a role play, think about the person you are speaking to, before planning the language you are going to use.

Try to imagine how much the patient might know about his or her condition. Imagine how much medical terminology the patient may understand, before assessing whether you should use medical terms or everyday terms.

Develop your own bank of expressions which you can use to explain symptoms, tests and treatment.

*Jaundice **makes you sleepy.***

*Jaundice **gives your skin a yellow tinge.***

*The blood tests **checks your bilirubin level.***

*The special light therapy **helps to lower your bilirubin.***

Reinforcing the importance of treatment

In order to reinforce the importance of treatment, you need to give patients strong advice, rather than make suggestions.

Suggested expressions:

It's essential, that you...

You must..../ You mustn't...

You really should..

Communication Focus: Persuading

To persuade a patient to do something, you have to explain why it is important, then ask for co-operation from the patient.

Some examples of role plays, where the nurse persuades the patient to do something:

- patient needs to remain in hospital for observation after a head injury
- patient needs to have a tetanus injection after an injury or dog bite
- patient needs to wait for blood results to see, if treatment is needed

- patient needs to take some medication
- patient needs to see the doctor, before leaving hospital

Steps to take, when persuading

Step 1. Explain the importance of doing something. Make sure you can explain in simple terms why something is important. E.g.

It's important that you have a tetanus injection after a dog bite. That's because you have more risk of getting tetanus which is a serious illness.

It's really important to have this injection, to prevent a serious infection.

Try to avoid **hesitant language** such as *'I think'*... You need to sound as if you know exactly what you are talking about. It's quite natural to use 'fillers' like *'Um'*, *'Mm, OK'* etc, but try not to overuse them.

Use positive rather than negative language. Try not to sound critical by using expressions such, *'You're wrong about this'* or *'No, that's not right at all.'* It's better to use positive language such as *'Yes, I understand what you mean but…'* or *'I agree with what you're saying, however, it's important to….'*

2. Reinforce the importance of the action, if the patient refuses to co-operate.
I understand that you have concerns about this, but I must stress how important this injection is.

3. Try to see the patient's point of view, if the patient refuses again. Accept that the patient has a right to refuse, but try to 'keep the door open', in case of a change of mind.
I appreciate what you're saying and I respect your right to refuse the injection. Would you be willing to read the information in this leaflet and come back if you change your mind?

Language Focus: Common illnesses

Many common illnesses are **uncountable.**

- childhood illnesses (*measles, chicken pox, diphtheria*)
- aches (*earache, toothache, stomach ache, backache*)
- disorders ending in 'ia' (*anaemia, pneumonia*)
- disorders ending in 'itis' (*hepatitis, appendicitis*)
- *cancer*
- *influenza* (but, not *'the flu'*)
- some acronyms (AIDS, BSE)

The symptoms of diseases are often **countable.**

- *a cold, the common cold*
- *a runny nose*
- *a cough*
- *a sore throat*
- *a headache*
- *a rash*
- *a fever*
- *the flu* (not *'a flu'*)
- *aches* (in particular) (*an earache, a stomach ache, a toothache, a backache*)

Activity 1: Watch the video at

https://www.youtube.com/watch?v=KBRHT8iccVg

and complete the words that the nurse uses.

1. Hello Serena. _____, but your baby still has a bit of jaundice and needs a blood test.

2. _____, but it depends on the amount of jaundice a baby has.

3. Bilirubin is made when _____.

4. _____. Can you tell me how your baby is feeding?

5. Babies can _____, that they don't wake easily to have a feed.

6. I'm sorry, Serena. _____ and you want to take your baby home, but he was quite small when he was born and he's feeding very slowly.

7. No, that wouldn't be a good idea. _____ _____, in case he needs treatment.

8. _____. We take precautions before babies go under the UV light.

9. _____, until the blood test results come back?

10. I'll let you know, _____ and we'll see if your baby needs the phototherapy or not.

Activity 2: Watch the video again and identify what the nurse is doing in sentences 1-10. Place a number next to the correct language function:

	giving strong advice about keeping baby in hospital
	explaining baby's appearance
	asking for co-operation
	assuring mother about getting test results as soon as possible
	explaining effect of jaundice on babies
	empathising about staying in hospital for blood test results
	appreciating mother's concerns, before asking about feeding
	empathising about need to keep baby in hospital
	appreciating mother's point of view about phototherapy
	explaining bilirubin in simple terms

Gathering information: Acute Back Pain

Scenario: Accident and Emergency Admission of Back

Vocabulary: Describing Pain

The McGill Pain Questionnaire is an assessment tool used to help patients describe what their pain feels like. Patients circle one word in each group that describes their pain. In the end, patients have seven words that describe the quality and intensity of their pain. This helps the physician to identify the most appropriate pain relief for them.

Some of the words are commonly used in collocations, e.g. *a throbbing headache.*

Sometimes patients add an additional explanation, e.g. *It's a stabbing pain. It feels, as if a knife is going into my side.*

Ongoing study hint: as you hear or read pain collocations, add them to a list in your note book. Put the words in a sentence to help remember them in context,

Group	Sensory Words: what the pain feels like physically
1	flickering, pulsing, quivering, throbbing, beating, pounding
2	jumping, flashing, shooting
3	pricking, boring, drilling, stabbing
4	sharp, cutting, lacerating
5	pinching, pressing, gnawing, cramping, crushing
6	tugging, pulling, wrenching
7	hot, burning, scalding, searing
8	tingling, itchy, smarting, stinging
9	dull, sore, hurting, aching, heavy
10	tender, taut, rasping, splitting

Group	Affective Words: emotions felt, because of pain
11	tiring, exhausting
12	sickening, suffocating
13	fearful, frightful, terrifying
14	punishing, gruelling, cruel, vicious, killing
15	wretched, blinding

Group	**Evaluative Words:** to estimate pain intensity
16	annoying, troublesome, miserable, intense, unbearable

Group	**Miscellaneous Words**
17	spreading, radiating, penetrating, piercing
18	tight, numb, squeezing, drawing, tearing
19	cool, cold, freezing
20	nagging, nauseating, agonizing, dreadful, torturing

Activity 1: Describing Pain

Select words from the tables above to complete the sentences.

1. I have a _____ headache. It feels, as if the pain turns on and off like a light.

2. The pain is _____. It makes me feel like I want to be sick.

3. I've got a _____ pain in my tooth. It's like a drill making a hole in my tooth.

4. I think I'm having a heart attack! I've got a _____ pain in the centre of my chest.

5. I haven't been able to eat for three days and now I've got a _____ pain in my stomach.

6. The pain is not severe, but it's a _____ pain that is always there.

7. I get severe _____ pains, when I have my period.

8. I've got a _____ pain in my ankle after I twisted it falling over.

9. I've got sciatica which is causing a _____ pain along the back of my legs.

10. I think my arthritis is getting worse, because I have a _____ ache in my knees in the mornings.

Scenario: Admission to A&E with Back Pain

Communication Strategies in the Role Play

- gathering information about back pain
- empathising but remaining firm
- encouraging to remain for assessment

Role Play Themes:

- back pain injury
- pain assessment using a pain scale
- pain management
- explaining procedure

Before you look at the nurse's role play card, think about the language you might use in the role play. Write down some ideas here.

Now, look at the role play card.

Setting: A&E

Nurse: You are talking to a patient who has come to A&E with severe **back pain.** She is insisting that you give her strong pain killers, so she can go home.

Task:

1. Ask for information about her pain (severity, type and location)

2. Explain a pain scale to the patient

3. Explain need for further investigations, before pain relief is given.

4. Empathise and reinforce importance of waiting to be checked by A&E doctor, before going home.

Communication Strategies used in the Role Play
Asking about Pain Using a Pain Scale

During the role play, the nurse asks the patient to rate the intensity of her pain after the patient tells her that the pain is 'really awful'.

Because pain is subjective, it is what a person says it is. It is therefore important to be able to understand the level of pain experienced.

Pain scales which are numeric use numbers to explain how intense pain is. The numbers run from zero to ten. Zero is the absence of pain, while ten is the worst pain experienced.

Pain scales are used for adults and children 10 years or older. Look at the table below for an indication of what the numbers in the scale mean.

Rating	Pain Level
0	no pain
1 – 3	mild pain nagging or annoying pain
4 – 6	moderate pain interferes with ability to perform daily activities
7 – 10	severe pain disabling, unable to perform daily activities

Communication Focus: Asking about Pain

Can you rate your pain on a scale from zero to ten?

Can you tell me what your pain is like on a scale from zero to ten?

Can you tell me about your pain on a scale from zero to ten?

Answers to Questions about Pain

0	I haven't got any pain.
	I don't have any pain.
	I'm pain-free at the moment.
Mild	It's just a nagging/niggling pain.
	I've only got a bit of pain.
	I've got a small amount of pain.
	It's mild.
Moderate	It's quite bad.
	It hurts quite a bit.
	It's fairly / pretty bad.
	It's moderate pain.
Severe	It's really bad.
	It is agonising.
	It's excruciating.
	It's killing me!
	It's terrible.
	It's so bad I can't stand it!

Activity 2: Watch the video at
https://www.youtube.com/watch?v=JzKhJJ28B98
and place what the nurse says about pain in order.

asks about type of pain

confirms pain worse on movement

asks if pain is a sharp pain or dull ache

asks about location of pain

asks patient to rate pain on a pain scale

Pain Management

During the role play, the patient tries to obtain strong pain relief. The nurse explains tactfully, that the patient will have to be assessed by the A&E doctor first.

Activity 3: Complete the steps the nurse takes.
Step 1: The nurse apologies and explains that he needs the patient to rate her pain.
Patient: Look, can you give me something for the pain. I really can't stand it!

Nurse: _____,
but I need to get a clear picture about the pain. Do you think you could rate your pain on a pain scale for me?

Step 2: The nurse empathises and tries to persuade the patient to stay and be assessed by the A&E doctor.
Patient: Yeah, I'd say my pain is an eight. Please. I really want something for the pain now.
Nurse: _____,
but I'll have to ask you to wait a bit longer. The Emergency Doctor will need to examine you first.

Step 3: Empathises, but firmly insists the patient stays to be seen by the doctor.
Patient: I don't need an X-ray. But I really need strong pain killers. I need to get home to my kids. Can't you just give me something now, so I can go home?
Nurse: _____, when you are in a lot of pain, but I'm afraid that you'll have to be seen by the doctor first.

Explaining a Procedure

The nurse explains what will happen, while the patient is in A&E. The explanation has three parts. Using no more than three points makes it easier to manage an explanation.

Activity 4: Watch the video again and answer the questions.

1. How does the nurse explain the A&E admission procedure?

A. prescribe painkillers, consult with doctor, X-ray

B. examine patient, check X-ray, talk about painkillers

C. X-ray patient, painkillers to take home, consult doctor

2. Why doesn't the nurse give the patient some painkillers?

A   nurses are not allowed to prescribe medication

B   the nurse is concerned about the patient

C   the nurse thinks the patient does not need them.

Scenario: High Cholesterol

Vocabulary

cholesterol

high risk

lifestyle changes

statins

Communication Strategies in the Role Play
- starting the role play
- gathering information
- explaining risk factors
- advising lifestyle changes
- encouraging a change of perspective

Role Play Themes:
- high cholesterol levels
- risk factors for heart disease
- management of high cholesterol
- lifestyle changes

Look at the nurse's role play card now.

Setting: Occupational Health Nurse Office

Nurse: You are talking to an employee, James Sutton, after a workplace health check showed he has high cholesterol levels. The employee has been asked to discuss the health check with you. You are going to explain the risks of high cholesterol in high risk groups and suggest some lifestyle changes the employee could make.

Tasks :

1. Find out what the employee already knows about high cholesterol.
2. Ask about past family history of heart disease.
3. Ask about employee's diet and exercise.
4. Give advice about important lifestyle changes to lower cholesterol levels.

Communication Focus: Starting the Role Play

Notice that the setting of the role play is the Occupational Health Nurse Office. The role play card tells you that the employee has been asked to come and see you to discuss his health check.

This means that the nurse knows why the employee is there, so there is no need for the type of opening question which might be asked in Accident and Emergency, for example. In the hospital setting, after an introduction, the nurse is likely to ask:

Can you tell me why you've come here today?

Can you tell me more about your injury?

In this case, the nurse introduces herself and explains why the employee was asked to see her.

Hello Mr Sutton. I'm Judy, the Occupational Health I asked you to come in and see me about your annual health report.

Some examples of role plays, which may use this sort of opening are:

- Parent is asked to see the School Nurse about child
- Employee visits Occupational Health Nurse to ask for medication
- High School student visits School Nurse to discuss health problem
- Relative of nursing home resident is called into to discuss changes in resident's health
- Relative of patient asks to speak to nurse in charge to make a complaint

Look at task 1 in the role play card. The first task is to find out what the employee already knows about high cholesterol. This is a useful question, because it can lead to a few different communication opportunities for the nurse. For instance,

1. The employee may not know anything about high cholesterol. This gives the nurse the opportunity to **explain the condition** and **give advice** on management.

2. The employee may say that he has read a lot about the condition on the internet, but may indicate that the information which was accessed on the internet is not accurate. This gives the nurse the opportunity to **be tactful** about explaining the importance of accessing accurate information and **encourage** the employee to get information which is specific to his needs.

3. The employee may have some understanding about the condition, but need more comprehensive information. This gives the nurse the opportunity to **confirm information** and **explain further.**

Gathering Information

The nurse uses both **open** and **closed questions** to gather information.

Closed questions are often used, when short answers or facts are required. For example,

*When did the pain start? (**Answer:** Yesterday)*

*How long have you had diabetes? (**Answer:** About 5 years)*

In this role play, the nurse wants to find out about the employee's family history of heart disease or stroke. The nurse wants specific information, not the employee's complete family medical history. She therefore asks,

What about your family? Is there anyone in your family with heart disease or who has had a stroke?

Open questions can be used to encourage patients to speak more about a topic, talk about their feelings or to give added detail to what is already known.

Open questions are also useful, when asking about sensitive topics. In this role play, the nurse wants to know about the employee's diet and whether he does any exercise.

If the nurse had asked : *Do you have a good diet?* and *Do you do any exercise?,* the employee may have felt that the nurse was being critical of his habits.

Instead, the nurse asked an open question, *Can you tell me a bit about your diet and how much exercise you do at present?*

Explaining Risk Factors

Having risk factors for a disease means possibly having a greater chance of developing the disease. Risk factors may include:

- having family members who have the same disease
- having a specific gene which is linked to the disease, e.g. the BRCA gene for breast cancer
- belonging to a racial group with a high risk of developing the disease
- having unhealthy lifestyle habits, e.g. smoking, misusing drugs or alcohol, eating to excess

- being a particular gender, i.e. male or female
- being a particular age, e.g. over 70 years old

Language used to explain risk factors

There are two main language areas you will use, when explaining risk factors to a patient.

1. Using 'may/might/could' to indicate possibilities

Because the presence of a risk factor does not guarantee the development of a disease, but makes it more likely, you should use the words, **could, may** and **might** to indicate possibility. E.g.

You might develop a chest infection.
You may be more likely to develop breast cancer.
You could have a greater chance of getting heart disease.

2. Using the expressions 'more likely to / greater chance of' to indicate consequences of risk factors

If you have these risk factors, you are more likely to develop breathing problems.

If you are over 60, you have a greater chance of developing joint problems.

Talking about Lifestyle Changes

In this role play, a health check identified that the employee has a high cholesterol level.

Cholesterol is a fatty substance which is vital for the normal functioning of the body. It is mainly made by the liver but can also be found in some foods. Having an excessively high level of lipids in your blood (called *hyperlipidaemia*) can have a negative effect on a person's health. High cholesterol levels do not cause any symptoms by themselves, but can increase the risk of serious health conditions, like heart disease. It is of particular concern, if a patient has other risk factors for heart disease or stroke.

The nurse gives advice about making lifestyle changes to lower the employee's cholesterol levels.

Some examples of topics in role plays, where lifestyle changes may be suggested are:
- obesity contributing to other health problems, e.g. strain on joints in arthritis
- smoking contributing to other health problems, e.g. diabetic ulcers, peripheral artery disease, chest infections
- moderate to heavy alcohol intake contributing to other health problems, e.g. sleep apnoea, depression
- poor diet contributing to other health problems, e.g. iron-deficiency anaemia, scurvy

Using 'non-judgemental' language

When giving advice on making lifestyle changes, it is important not to sound, as though you are being critical about a patient, that is **judging** them for having make unwise decisions about their health.

Levels of Advice

In role plays, where the nurses give advice to a patient or carer, it is important to think about the type of advice to be given. It may range from a suggestion to strong advice. Examples of language include:

Empathising first:

I know that it might seem difficult to give up smoking, but...
I imagine that it must seem hard to try to....

Suggestions

It would be a good idea to make some lifestyle changes.
You should think about making some changes to your diet.
It would be beneficial if you could do some exercise.

Advice

Try to start by eating smaller portions.
You need to do at least 30 minutes exercise each week.

Strong advice

It's important that you take your statins every day. (this is not a suggestion – she is telling him something which is important)

Encouraging patients to consider a change

Would you be willing to make some changes in your diet?

Do you think you might start walking a few times a week?

Do you think that you could start walking a few times a week?

Watch the YouTube video at

https://www.youtube.com/watch?v=MpbeaYpg4sc

Activity 1: Put the notes in the order that you hear them.

The nurse:

introduces herself

explains results of health check

asks what employee understands about condition

explains when high cholesterol is a problem

explains high risk factors

explains necessity of making lifestyle changes

explains effect of statins in context of lifestyle changes

advises benefits of exercise programme

advises discussion with GP about statins

Activity 2: Complete the questions and sentences from the dialogue.

1. Can you tell me what _____?
2. High cholesterol levels are a concern when they _____.

3. Is there anyone in your family with heart disease or _____?

4. Smoking is another risk factor _____.

5. Can you tell me a bit about your diet and how much _____?

6. I'm afraid it is essential that _____.

7. Taking a statin will lower the amount of cholesterol in your body, but you'll still _____.

8. Are you willing to think about _____?

9. It would also be beneficial _____.

10. Would you consider getting into _____?

Activity 3: Place the numbers from the previous activity under the correct headings. The first one is done for you.

Asking for information	1,
Explaining a condition	
Giving advice	
Persuading	

Scenario: Diabetic Foot Injury

Vocabulary

amputation

diabetes

infected

nerve damage

Communication Strategies in the Role Play

- allaying anxiety
- confirming understanding of information
- managing misinformation
- explaining treatment

Role Play Themes:

- diabetic injuries
- health information on the internet
- wound care

Allaying anxiety

The patient in this role play explains that she accidentally cut herself, while walking on the beach. She is very concerned now, as the wound looks infected and she knows this may be serious, as she has diabetes. The nurse tries to lessen the patient's anxiety, after hearing why the patient is worried.

Other role plays which may include an element of anxiety felt by the patient include role plays with:

- a parent of a sick child
- a patient waiting for a test result to confirm cancer diagnosis
- a patient anxious about an operation

Allaying Anxiety: Reassuring Patients

It is generally understood that patients who receive no reassurance or ineffective reassurance do not recover as well as patients who receive positive and realistic reassurance.

In order to reassure a patient, the first step is to acknowledge that you understand why they are upset or worried. If you do not so this, it may seem that you are making excuses or are too busy to listen to them.

When reassuring patients, it is essential that you do not tell them, that 'everything will be all right.' Examples of role plays, where this would be particularly inappropriate are
role plays which deal with a possible diagnosis of cancer, e.g. a woman waiting for a biopsy result or role plays about a possible admission to a Nursing Home, e.g. an elderly person who is struggling to cope at home).

What not to say:
'Don't worry. It will be OK.' (How do you know that?)
' Things always turn out in the end.' (But maybe they don't turn out in a satisfactory way)
'We are only sent as much as we can cope with.' (Perhaps but many people are unable to cope well if they are already under stress)

'Everything will be fine, you'll see.' (Fine for whom and if it isn't?)

'It's only a small procedure; nothing to worry about' (But it may be to the patient)

Nurses who dismiss a patient's concerns with a clichéd reassurance *('Don't worry. It will be OK')* can actually increase the patient's stress and anxiety levels. They also damage the trust between nurse and patient which may be difficult to rebuild.

Steps to Take to Reassure Patients

Step 1: Acknowledge the patient's concerns.

I can see that you are upset about this.
I can imagine that you are concerned about this.
I appreciate that this has been very frightening for you.

Step 2: Reassure the patient.

Try to reassure the patient by providing information, explaining that the concerns are natural or by reinforcing that the patient has taken the correct action. Remember that if you are giving a patient information, be aware of the amount of information patients are able to take in. Confirm understanding every so often.

Make sure your verbal reassurance (the words) matches your non-verbal reassurance (your body language). It is important that your verbal and non-verbal reassurances are consistent with your actions (and the later actions of other healthcare practitioners). This is called being **congruent.**

If you reassure a patient that 'all is well', but then say that the patient needs a blood test, 'to check that everything is OK', the patient will feel confused and not reassured at all. This is called being **incongruent.**

Finally, be conscious of the fact that you will probably not be able to reassure a highly anxious patient. It is therefore not recommended, that you try to reassure a patient who is already anxious. Other communication strategies are more appropriate.

Examples of statements used to reassure:

1. Providing information

I can see, that you are nervous about the operation. I'll explain exactly what is going to happen tomorrow, so you will know what to expect. **(**Many patients feel relieved, if they know what to expect before an operation.)

2. Explaining that the concerns are natural

I can see that you are upset about this. Actually, it's quite normal to have some concerns before you start the treatment. Would you like to talk to about it with me now?

3. Reinforcing that the patient has taken the correct action

I can see that you are upset about this. But, you did the right thing bringing your husband into hospital as quickly as you did.

Using expressions like 'Try not to worry'

Use the expression *'Try not to worry'*, rather than *'Don't worry.'*

I can see that you are upset about this. **Try not to worry.** *You did the right thing by bringing your husband into hospital as quickly as you did.*

I imagine that you are nervous about the operation. **Try not to worry.** *I'll explain exactly what is going to happen tomorrow, so you will know what to expect. Most people feel relieved if they know what to expect before an operation.*

Confirming Information

During the role play, the nurse is unsure about something the patient says. The nurse makes sure that she checks what the patient really meant to say. This is because it is always important to understand exactly what patients say. It can make a difference to patient safety.

Patient: …. If I hadn't checked my toe this morning, I would never have known that there was a problem. Now I'm worried that it's too late!

Nurse: I imagine that it must be difficult for you, always being on alert for cuts and injuries. **But I'm not sure that I understand what you mean by it being too late.**

Managing Misinformation

During the role play, the patient explains that she had looked on the internet for information about diabetic injuries. She became concerned about diabetic amputations. The nurse tactfully explains that looking for health information on the internet can be helpful, but it may be better to consult with the patient's diabetes specialist.

Patients who say that they have obtained information from other sources, e.g. the internet, friends or relatives, can be used as a method of distracting the nurse.

Other role plays which may use this method:

- the patient insists on having the same medication as her friend, who has the same condition
- the patient says he has information about a forthcoming operation from the internet
- the patient refuses treatment, because a relative gives her information from an internet health website

Explaining Treatment

Treatment explained during nursing role plays may include:

- having tests, e.g. ECGs , X-rays or blood tests
- wound care, e.g. doing a dressing
- administration of medication, e.g. intravenous therapy (an IV or 'drip'), eye drops or inhalers
- a plaster cast

Study Hint: Keep a record of common treatments in your note book. Group relevant expressions with each example, e.g.

wound dressings
- clean the wound / put on a sterile dressing / secure the dressing with tape
- keep the dressing clean and dry / have the stitches out in a week

intravenous antibiotics (IV antibiotics)
- go through the vein, so they work faster / need to have antibiotics through the vein to work faster

plaster cast
- keep the cast dry / don't poke anything sharp under the cast / report tingling of the fingers

Activity 1: Explaining diabetes complications

Match the medical terms relating to diabetes complications with their everyday equivalent terms.

1. retinopathy	a. kidney disease
2. neuropathy	b. high blood glucose level
3. nephropathy	c. nerve damage
4. amputation	d. low blood glucose levels
5. hyperglycaemia	e. surgical removal of a limb
6. hypoglycaemia	f. vision problems

Activity 2: Watch the video at

https://www.youtube.com/watch?v=kHNOWt5uN4I

Identify the sentences the nurse uses to lessen the patient's anxiety.

1. I see from your notes that you're a bit concerned about a cut on your foot.

2. OK, well you did the right thing coming in to have it checked.

3. You did the right thing coming to hospital, as soon as you did.

4. I imagine that it must be difficult for you, always being on alert for cuts and injuries.

5. It's good to be informed about your diabetes, but it's also important to talk to your diabetes doctor or nurse, if you're worried about something like this.

6. The first thing I'll do is take a look at the cut and put a new dressing on it.

7. No, it's better to use special dressings, rather than plasters.

Activity 3: What did the nurse say to indicate that she didn't understand, what the patient meant?

A   I didn't catch what you meant by that.

B   I didn't understand about you being late.

C   I'm not sure that I understand what you mean by it being too late.

Activity 4: What do these terms mean?

1. on alert for
2. a drip
3. a protective boot
4. be informed about

Activity 5: Put the steps of the explanation of treatment in the order you hear them.

	possible antibiotics
	protective boot until cut heals
	look at the cut
	possible intravenous antibiotics
	put on a dressing
	see the diabetes doctor at Outpatients
	dressing change in Outpatients

Transcripts
Child with Eczema
https://www.youtube.com/watch?v=i3LXUvS1llU

Scenario: Child with Eczema

Nurse: Hello, I'm George. I'm one of the nurses in A&E. Your daughter's having problems with her eczema. Is that right?

Patient: Yes. She's got a lot of problems with her skin at the moment. She just scratches most of the time. She even finds it hard to sleep, because it's so itchy.

Nurse: Can you tell me about your daughter's current treatment? Do you use creams on the eczema?

Patient: Yes. Well, sometimes. The GP gave me some cream to use every day. It's like a moisturiser.

Nurse: That's good. It's very important to use moisturisers a few times a day. When do you usually put the cream on?

Patient: I put it on first thing in the morning after she has a bath. Then a couple of times during the day if she is itching a lot. I try to put it on last thing at night. Before she goes to bed.

Nurse: It sounds like you are doing the right thing with the moisturiser. Can you tell me again how often you give your daughter a bath?

Patient: I give her a bath every morning, so she is clean for the day. I'm always careful to use unperfumed soap. It's supposed to be better for her skin.

Nurse: Yes, it's better to use unperfumed soap, if you have a skin condition like eczema, but it might be better for your daughter not to have a bath every day. Hot water tends to dry out the skin.

Patient: Even if I use a moisturiser afterwards?

Nurse: That's right, hot water can be very drying. What about other creams? Are you using any other creams apart from the moisturiser?

Patient: Well, I'm supposed to use a steroid cream, if her skin gets very red and inflamed. The thing is, I don't want to use the steroid cream. I don't think it's safe.

Nurse: I can appreciate your concerns. Many people worry about steroid creams, because they think it's like the steroids that weight lifters use.

Patient: Yes, that's what I thought.

Nurse: Actually, the cream your GP suggested has a very low dose of steroid medication in it. You only use the cream, when the eczema flares up, because it's only a short-term treatment.

Patient: I'm still not happy about it. I was reading about some natural creams on the internet. They're supposed to be very good.

Nurse: Some of these creams can be very good, but it's important to remember that they still contain medications. Your GP has prescribed a cream that she thinks is right for your daughter. And it's only to be used now and then, when the condition gets worse. It's important to stop severe itching that may lead to the skin bleeding.

Patient: Oh dear, maybe that's why her skin is in such a bad state! It became very red and extremely itchy last week. She was scratching all the time. Then some of the areas on both her arms started to bleed. Now they're weeping and I'm worried that it's infected.

Nurse: I can see that it's very difficult for you, but you did the right thing coming here to have your daughter checked out. If her skin is infected, your daughter may need to take a course of antibiotics, until the infection clears.

Patient: I see. What can I do to prevent this happening again?

Nurse: I've brought a patient information leaflet for you. It has some very good hints about the management of eczema.

Patient: Thanks. That sounds very helpful.

Nurse: There are things you can do at home, to make your daughter more comfortable. Try to keep her cool, especially at night. It may make it easier for her to sleep. Also, it would be better to dress your daughter in clothes made of cotton or natural fibres.

Patient: OK. Is there anything else I can do?

Nurse: Yes. It would be a good idea to cut down on the number of baths your daughter has, to prevent her skin from drying out. It's essential that you put on the moisturising cream several times a day. Keeping the skin moisturised is one way you can help to prevent skin infections.

Patient: OK. So, few baths and keep her skin well moisturised.

Nurse: Finally, use the steroid cream for flareups and only as a short-term treatment.

Patient: Yes, I see. I understand now, that there are times when my daughter may need the steroid cream.

Nurse: That's right. Everything we talked about is in the leaflet. Take it home with you and call us, if you have any further questions.

Patient: I'll do that. Thank you for the advice.

Baby with Jaundice

https://www.youtube.com/watch?v=KBRHT8iccVg

Scenario: Young Mother and Baby with Jaundice

Patient: Nurse, I was supposed to go home today. I want to take my baby home.

Nurse: Hello Serena. I know you don't want to be here, but your baby still has a bit of jaundice and needs a blood test.

Patient: Yeah. OK, he's a bit yellow, but he's not sick. My friend's baby had jaundice and she took him home. Why can't I take my baby home?

Nurse: I know he looks all right, but it depends on the amount of jaundice a baby has. That's why your baby needs a blood test.

Patient: I don't really understand about it. Is jaundice dangerous?

Nurse: Jaundice is a condition which happens when there is too much of a chemical called bilirubin in the baby's body. Bilirubin is made when old red blood cells break down. Many newborns are not able to clear the extra bilirubin for a couple of weeks. The yellow colour of the skin is a sign that your baby has jaundice.

Patient: But is it dangerous?

Nurse: It's not usually dangerous in newborns. Most cases clear up by themselves in a couple of weeks. But, some babies need a bit of treatment to clear the jaundice.

Patient: OK, but my baby looks all right. I really want to take him home.

Nurse: I can appreciate that. Can you tell me how your baby is feeding?

Patient: I'm breast feeding him.

Nurse: Sorry, I meant, whether your son wakes up to have his feeds.

Patient: Oh, OK. Sometimes it's hard to wake him up to give him a feed.

Nurse: That sometimes happens when babies have jaundice. Babies can become so sleepy, that they don't wake easily to have a feed or they feed very slowly.

Patient: Oh OK. What's going to happen now?

Nurse: First, it's great that you're breast feeding. Keep breastfeeding and don't supplement the feeds or give your baby water in between feeds.

Patient: I thought I had to give him water, in case he's thirsty.

Nurse: In this case, breast milk is all your baby needs, to help clear the jaundice.

Patient: So, we can go home then?

Nurse: I'm sorry, Serena. I know it's hard for you and you want to take your baby home, but he was quite small when he was born and he's feeding very slowly. It's important to wait for the results of his blood test to see if he needs some treatment for the jaundice.

Patient: Can't I just wait for the blood test results at home?

Nurse: No, that wouldn't be a good idea. It's better, if your baby stays here, in case he needs treatment.

Patient: What kind of treatment?

Nurse: It's quite simple. We just use a special light over the baby in his crib. It's a UV light which helps to break down bilirubin, until your baby can do it himself.

Patient: I'm not sure I like that idea. It sounds dangerous.

Nurse: I understand your concerns. We take precautions before babies go under the UV light. We also cover their eyes while they're under the light and time the sessions. The other thing we do, is make sure that the babies have enough water to prevent dehydration.

Patient: OK, I see. I'm still not happy about staying in here though. I just want to go home.

Nurse: I know it's not like home in hospital. Would you be willing to stay in hospital, until the blood test results come back? It's really very important.

Patient: Yes, I understand all that. I suppose I can wait a bit for the blood test results.

Nurse: That's great, Serena. I'll let you know, as soon as I get the results and we'll see if your baby needs the phototherapy or not.

Acute Back Pain
https://www.youtube.com/watch?v=JzKhJJ28B98

Scenario: Acute Back Pain

Nurse: Hello, I'm Andy, one of the nurses on duty today. I see in your notes that you've come in with some back pain. Is that right?

Patient: Yes, I've got terrible back pain. I can hardly stand it.

Nurse: All right. I need to ask a few questions about the pain, if that's OK.

Patient: I suppose so. Yeah, OK.

Nurse: Can you tell me where the pain is, and what it feels like?

Patient: Well, it's mostly in my lower back. You know, right across my back. The pain's really awful. It hurts a lot, especially when I try to move.

Nurse: OK. What type of pain is it? Is it a sharp pain or a dull ache for example?

Patient: It's a sharp pain. It feels like a knife in my back, when I try to move.

Nurse: Right, so a sharp pain in your lower back which is worse, if you try to move.

Patient: Look, can you give me something for the pain. I really can't stand it!

Nurse: I'm sorry to ask all these questions, but I need to get a clear picture about the pain. Do you think you could rate your pain on a pain scale for me? On a scale between zero meaning no pain and ten meaning the worst pain, that you've ever experienced.

Patient: Oh. I don't know. It's really bad, but I am not sure which number it is.

Nurse: One to three is mild pain, a niggling pain that's a bit annoying. Four to six is moderate pain, that's enough to interfere with your daily activities. Severe pain is bad enough to stop you from moving around . Most people rate this sort of pain between seven and ten.

Patient: Yeah, I'd say my pain is an eight. Please. I really want something for the pain now.

Nurse: I can see that the pain is really bad, but I'll have to ask you to wait a bit longer. The Emergency Doctor will need to examine you first. You might have an X-ray to check for any damage to your spine. Then the doctor will talk to you about some pain killers to take home.

Patient: I don't need an X-ray. But I really need strong pain killers. I need to get home to my kids. Can't you just give me something now, so I can go home?

Nurse: I understand that it is very difficult when you are in a lot of pain, but I'm afraid that you'll have to be seen by the doctor first. It's important to check that you haven't injured yourself, before giving you any painkillers.

Patient: This is ridiculous! I may as well go to the pharmacy and get something there. I think I'll just go home. I'm not getting any help here at all.

Nurse: I can see that it might seem, as though you aren't getting any help. Now that I've asked you those questions about the pain, I'll ask the Emergency doctor to come and see you. Would you be willing to wait, until she talks to you?

Patient: Well, I guess I don't have much choice. Yeah, OK I'll wait a bit longer.

Nurse: That's great. I'll see, if she's available to see you now.

High Cholesterol
https://www.youtube.com/watch?v=MpbeaYpg4sc

Scenario: High Cholesterol

Nurse: Hello Mr Sutton. I'm Judy, the Occupational Health I asked you to come in and see me about your annual health report. It showed up a few things which we should talk about

Patient: Yes, I thought there might be a few issues.

Nurse: Your cholesterol level is quite high and so is your blood pressure. Can you tell me what you know about high cholesterol?

Patient: Well, I don't know very much. I've read a bit about taking medication to lower cholesterol levels, but I don't really know why getting the levels down is so important.

Nurse: High cholesterol levels are a concern when they are combined with other risk factors and especially if you are in a high risk group for heart attack or stroke.

Patient: Oh, I see why everyone is worried now. How do I know if I'm in a high risk group?

Nurse: A family history of heart disease or stroke is one high risk group. What about your family? Is there anyone in your family with heart disease or who has had a stroke?

Patient: Yes. My father had a heart attack and died when I was quite young. It's not looking good. I have high blood pressure as well. At least I'm not a smoker.

Nurse: That is a good thing. Smoking is another risk factor for heart attack and stroke. However, having high blood pressure, high cholesterol and a family history of heart disease means that you have more chance of having a heart attack or stroke than someone who doesn't have these risk factors.

Patient: I see.

Nurse: Can you tell me a bit about your diet and how much exercise you do at present?

Patient: Well, I have to be honest with you. My diet isn't what it should be. I know that I should lose weight and do some exercise , but the trouble is I like a few beers, especially when I come home from work. Once I sit on the sofa and turn on the TV, that's as far as any exercise goes. My weight has increased a lot over the past year.

Nurse: Yes, It is hard to get out of a habit like that. I appreciate how difficult it is to make changes.

Patient: Do I really have to make any changes? Most of my friends are as overweight as I am, and they don't seem to have any problems.

Nurse: I'm afraid it is essential that you make some changes. The problem in your case is that you have several risk factors. You have a family history of cardiovascular disease, you have high blood pressure and high cholesterol. You are a bit overweight and you don't exercise enough.

Patient: What about taking tablets? I think they're called statins. Wouldn't they fix the problem?

Nurse: Taking a statin will lower the amount of cholesterol in your body, but you'll still need to manage the other risk factors. Are you willing to think about going on a weight loss programme?

Patient: I'm not really keen on the idea. I don't know. I'll have to think about it.

Nurse: I know it is a hard thing to do, but it is really important. It would also be beneficial to do some exercise.

Would you consider getting into an exercise programme as well?

Patient: Yes, I think so and I'll definitely make an effort to get my weight down too. I don't want to have a heart attack like my father!

Nurse: That's great. You should talk to your GP about taking statins as well.

Patient: Thanks, Judy. I'll do that.

Diabetic Foot Injury
https://www.youtube.com/watch?v=kHNOWt5uN4I
Scenario: Diabetic Injury

Nurse: Hello I'm Sandra, one of the nurses here in A&E. I see from your notes that you're a bit concerned about a cut on your foot.

Patient: Yes. That's right. I've got a cut on my little toe, on my right foot. I wouldn't be worried so much, except that I've got diabetes.

Nurse: OK, well you did the right thing coming in to have it checked. Can you tell me what happened?

Patient: I'm usually so careful about my feet. I went to the beach with some friends and we were walking a bit too close to the rocks. I slipped on a rock and cut my foot.

Nurse: I see. When did it happen?

Patient: It was yesterday just before lunch. I'm really worried about it now. I should have come in straight away, but I tried to clean it myself. When I woke up this morning, I noticed that my toe was red and swollen. It just didn't look right. I'm really worried that the cut's infected and I'll end up losing my toe!

Nurse: You did the right thing coming to hospital, as soon as you did. I can see that you understand how important it is to keep an eye on cuts, if you have diabetes.

Patient: I know, but I'm so angry with myself. I know that a cut probably won't be painful, because of the nerve damage with diabetes. If I hadn't checked my toe this morning, I would never have known that there was a problem. Now I'm worried that it's too late!

Nurse: I imagine that it must be difficult for you, always being on alert for cuts and injuries. But I'm not sure that I understand what you mean by it being too late.

Patient: Well, this morning I started getting worried about my toe, especially when I saw how red it was. I even looked it up on the internet and I found all this stuff about diabetic amputations. Now I'm terrified in case I end up losing my toe.

Nurse: I understand now. It's good to be informed about your diabetes, but it's also important to talk to your diabetes doctor or nurse, if you're worried about something like this. They know what's best for your particular situation.

Patient: What's going to happen now?

Nurse: The first thing I'll do is take a look at the cut and put a new dressing on it. Then the A & E doctor may prescribe some antibiotics to clear up any infection. You might need to have a drip to have the antibiotics, because they get into your bloodstream faster through your vein.

Patient: What about the dressing? Should I change the plaster myself?

Nurse: No, it's better to use special dressings, rather than plasters. You'll need to come into Outpatients to have the dressing changed every day, so we can check on it. I'll also give you a protective boot to wear, until the cut heals.

Patient: OK, right. I understand now. What about seeing the diabetes doctor?

Nurse: You'll see the diabetes doctor at Outpatients tomorrow. I'll make an appointment for you now.

Patient: Great. Thanks.

Answers
Scenario: Eczema
Activity 1: Complete the nurse's sentences:

1. Yes, <u>it's better to use</u> unperfumed soap, if you have a skin condition like eczema….

2. … but <u>it might be better</u> for your daughter not to have a bath every day.

3. Some of these creams can be very good, but <u>it's important to</u> remember that they still contain medications.

4. <u>It's important to</u> stop severe itching that may lead to the skin bleeding.

5. <u>Try to</u> keep her cool, especially at night. It may make it easier for her to sleep.

6. Also, <u>it would be better to</u> dress your daughter in clothes made of cotton or natural fibres.

7. <u>It would be a good idea to</u> cut down on the number of baths your daughter has…

8. <u>It's essential that you</u> put on the moisturising cream several times a day.

9. Finally, <u>use</u> the steroid cream for flareups and only as a short-term treatment.

10. <u>Take</u> it home with you and <u>call us</u>, if you have any further questions.

Activity 2: Patient Information Leaflet

1. Nurse

2. Nurse

3. Mother

4. Nurse

5. Nurse

6. Nurse

7. Nurse

8. Nurse

9.

10.

Scenario: Young Mother and Baby with Jaundice

Activity 1

1. Hello Serena. <u>I know you don't want to be here</u>, but your baby still has a bit of jaundice and needs a blood test.

2. <u>I know he looks all right</u>, but it depends on the amount of jaundice a baby has.

3. Bilirubin is made when <u>old red blood cells break down</u>.

4. <u>I can appreciate that.</u> Can you tell me how your baby is feeding?

5. Babies can <u>become so sleepy</u>, that they don't wake easily to have a feed

6. I'm sorry, Serena. <u>I know it's hard for you</u> and you want to take your baby home, but he was quite small when he was born and he's feeding very slowly.

7. No, that wouldn't be a good idea. <u>It's better, if your baby stays here</u>, in case he needs treatment.

8. <u>I understand your concerns.</u> We take precautions before babies go under the UV light.

9. <u>Would you be willing to stay in hospital</u>, until the blood test results come back?

10. I'll let you know, <u>as soon as I get the results</u> and we'll see if your baby needs the phototherapy or not.

Activity 2:

7	giving strong advice about keeping baby in hospital
2	explaining baby's appearance
9	asking for co-operation
10	assuring mother about getting test results as soon as possible
5	explaining effect of jaundice on babies
1	empathising about staying in hospital for blood test results
4	appreciating mother's concerns, before asking about feeding
6	empathising about need to keep baby in hospital
8	appreciating mother's point of view about phototherapy
3	explaining bilirubin in simple terms

Scenario: Back Pain
Activity 1: Describing Pain
Select words from the tables above to complete the sentences.

1. I have a <u>flickering</u> headache. It feels, as if the pain turns on and off like a light.

2. The pain is <u>nauseating.</u> It makes me feel like I want to be sick.

3. I've got a <u>boring</u> pain in my tooth. It's like a drill making a hole in my tooth.

4. I think I'm having a heart attack! I've got a <u>crushing</u> pain in the centre of my chest.

5. I haven't been able to eat for three days and now I've got a <u>gnawing</u> pain in my stomach.

6. The pain is not severe, but it's a <u>nagging</u> pain that is always there.

7. I get severe <u>cramping</u> pains, when I have my period.

8. I've got a <u>wrenching</u> pain in my ankle after I twisted it falling over.

9. I've got sciatica which is causing a <u>shooting</u> pain along the back of my legs.

10. I think my arthritis is getting worse, because I have a <u>dull</u> ache in my knees in the mornings.

Activity 2:

asks about location of pain

asks about type of pain

asks if pain is a sharp pain or dull ache

asks patient to rate pain on a pain scale

confirms pain worse on movement

Activity 3:

Step 1: I'm sorry to ask all these questions

Step 2: I can see that the pain is really bad

Step 3: I understand that it is very difficult

Activity 4:

1. B examine patient, check X-ray, talk about painkillers

2. A nurses are not allowed to prescribe medication

Scenario: High Cholesterol

Activity 1: Put the notes in the order that you hear them.

The nurse:

introduces herself

explains results of health check

asks what employee understands about condition

explains when high cholesterol is a problem

explains high risk factors

explains necessity of making lifestyle changes

explains effect of statins in context of lifestyle changes

advises benefits of exercise programme

advises discussion with GP about statins

Activity 2: Complete the questions and sentences from the dialogue.

1. Can you tell me what <u>you know about high cholesterol</u>?

2. High cholesterol levels are a concern when they <u>are combined with other risk factors</u>.

3. Is there anyone in your family with heart disease or <u>who has had a stroke</u>?

4. Smoking is another risk factor <u>for heart attack and stroke</u>.

5. Can you tell me a bit about your diet and how much <u>exercise you do at present</u>?

6. I'm afraid it is essential that <u>you make some changes</u>.

7. Taking a statin will lower the amount of cholesterol in your body, but you'll still <u>need to manage the other risk factors</u>.

8. Are you willing to think about <u>going on a weight loss programme</u>?

9. It would also be beneficial <u>to do some exercise</u>.

10. Would you consider getting into <u>an exercise programme as well</u>?

Activity 3.

Asking for information	1, 3, 5
Explaining a condition	2, 4
Giving advice	6, 7, 9
Persuading	8, 10

Scenario: Diabetic injury

Activity 1:

1.f   2.c   3.a   4.e   5.b   6.d

Activity 2:

2. OK, well you did the right thing coming in to have it checked.

3. You did the right thing coming to hospital, as soon as you did.

Activity 3:
C   But I'm not sure that I understand what you mean by it being too late.

Activity 4:

1. on alert for   be prepared for an emergency

2. a drip   intravenous therapy or IV

3. a protective boot   boot worn over to protect the foot from injury from sharp objects

4. be informed about   understand facts surrounding an issue

Activity 5:

3	possible antibiotics
6	protective boot until cut heals
1	look at the cut
4	possible intravenous antibiotics
2	put on a dressing
7	see the diabetes doctor at Outpatients
5	dressing change in Outpatients

Lightning Source UK Ltd.
Milton Keynes UK
UKHW02f0713250918
329483UK00013B/1536/P